AF583442

BFA ENTRANCE EXAM GUIDE

DEVESH TANEJA

Made with ♥ on the Notion Press Platform
www.notionpress.com

Contents

CHAPTER I

IMPORTANT FACT FILES

1. *Gitanjali is written by Rabindranath Tagore.*

2. *Ajanta paintings are related to Buddha.*

3. *Leonardo-da-Vinci's famous painting is Monalisa.*

4. *Blue is a cool color.*

5. *Ancient Indian art is inspired by religion.*

6. *Bharat muni described Rasa in his Natyashastra.*

7. *Abnindranath nath tagore discovered wash technique in India.*

8. *Gothic art is famous for window glass painting.*

9. Altamira caves belong to pre-historic period.

10 Ajanta has 30 caves(29 in some books).

11. The main subject of Raja Ravi Varma's painting is Hindu mythology.

12. Water colors are transparent.

13. Shantiniketan is situated in West Bengal.

14. Main centre of Pahari School of art is Kangra.

15. Tempera colours are used in Rajasthani Painting.

16. Bani Thani Belongs to Kishangarh.

17. Guernica was painted by Picasso.

18. In India 1st printing machine was established in 1556 at Goa.

19. Madhubani miniature style belongs to Bihar.

20. Shree Ram Janam Bhumi is Ayodhya.

21. NGMA(national gallery of modern art) is in Delhi.

22. Taj Mahal is built by king Shahajahan.

23. Taj Mahal is in Agra.

24. Canvas is the perfect surface for oil paintings.

25. There are 3 primary colours RED, YELLOW, BLUE.

26. Eiffel Tower is situated in France.

27. There are 7 colours in rainbow.

28. Leonardo-da-vinci painted Last Supper.

29. G. R. Santosh is related to Tantrik Art.

30. Byzantine art is famous for Mosaic Art.

31. M. F. Hussain is known for painting Horses.

32. Jan Van Eyck is known as the father of oil painting.

33. In printmaking planography is called Lithography.

34. Bani-Thani painting is painted by Nihal Chand.

35. Dhanraj Bhagat is a famous sculptor.

36. Prominent painter of Bengal school is Abanindranath

Tagore.

37. Kishangarh Miniature paintings are related to Rajasthan.

38. First newspaper was printed in Calcutta.

39. Bengal Gazette was first Indian printed newspaper.

40. Sare Jahan se Achaa was written by Muhammad Iqbal.

41. R. K. Laxman is a famous cartoonist.

42. Bismillah Khan is a Shahnai player.

43. J. J. School of art is in Mumbai.

44. Mount Everest is the highest Mountain in the world.

45. *The Bengal Gazette is the 1st Indian newspaper.*

46. *Lost wax technique is a casting process of Bronze.*

47. *Warli folk painting is related to Maharashtra.*

48. *Thick application of colour is called impasto.*

49. *Somnath Hore created the pulp print series "wounds".*

50. *Architect of Taj Mahal is Ustad Ahmad Lahouri.*

51. *Warm colors are yellow, red and orange.*

52. *Bihu is a folk dance of Assam.*

53. *In Indian flag saffron colour mean sacrifice and courage.*

54. Death of Shah-Jahan is painted by Abanindranth Tagore.

55. Bharat Mata is painted by Abanindranath Tagore.

56. "The persistence of memory" is painted by Salvador Dali.

57. Ram Kinkar Baij is a well-known sculptor.

58. Cheret was the poster designer.

59. Cezanne is called the father of modern art.

60. Raja Ravi Varma is called the father of Indian modern Art.

61. Graphite is a pencil lead.

62. Sculpture comes under 3D art and Painting comes under 2D art.

63. Poster in comparison to Hording is small.

64. In textile design block printing, roller printing and screen printing is included but Fresco painting is avoided.

64. During Jahangir's time best artist of "Birds" was Mansoor.

65. The quality of Bengal school is wash technique.

66. Michelangelo made the sculpture of "Pieta" in marble.

67. Famous rock-cut temple is in Ellora named "Kailashnath temple".

68. Monolithic sculpture of Bahubali is in Shravanabelagola, Karnata.

69. Terracotta warriors is found in China.

70. The inner eye documentary is made by "Satyajit Ray".

71. Where the First book was printed from wood block= China.

72. The National Emblem of India is based on The Ashokan lion capital at Sarnath.

73. Elephanta is famous for Trimurti.

74. The Sanchi Stupa is situated near Bhopal.

75. NIFT is an educational centre devoted to Fashion Technology.

76. One inch has 72 points.

77. The name of the cloth used in silk screen making is Bolting Cloth.

78. Letter press printing come under Relief process.

79. Which is not a material for Plastic art- Mercury.

80. Pongal is a Popular festival of Tamil Nadu.

81. Vande Matram is written by Bakim Chand.

82. Printing Press was invented by Jhon Gutten Berg.

83. Painting on paper was started in 14th century.

84. Bal Thakre started his earning as a cartoonist.

85. R. K. Laxman's Common Man is a famous Indian Cartoon.

86. Van Gogh cut his ear off & gifted it to His Beloved.

87. Rag-Ragini paintings were popularly painted in Rajasthan.

88. Geru color was mainly used in Prehistoric paintings.

89. Miniature paintings were started in Pala & Jain.

90. Logo is a stylised name of any product & company.

91. Radio ads with rhymes and music are known as Jingles.

92. Mechanical printing was started in India in 1556 in Goa.

93. Capital letters are known as Upper Case.

94. Original name of poster is Billboard.

95. In 1982 colour T.V was introduced in India.

96. Set Squares are Triangular.

97. Pandit Ravi Shankar is related to Sitar.

98. Bismillah Khan is known for Shehnai.

99. Kandaria Mahadev temple of Khajuraho belongs to Hinduism.

100. D. P. Roy Chaudhary is a sculptor.

101. The ratio of Indian flag Width to Length is 2:3.

102. The ratio of Indian flag Length to Width is 3:2.

CHAPTER II

VERY SHORT QUESTION AWNSERS

Q1. The National Bird of India is:
Ans. Peacock

Q2. Tiger Woods is a famous:
Ans. Golfer

Q3. Diego Maradona was a famous:
Ans. Football Player

Q4. Which country has largest population in the world?
Ans. China

Q5. Which state is famous for Tea?
Ans. Assam

Q6. Shivaji was the ruler of:
Ans. Maratha

Q7. Tansen the famous musician was in the court of which Mughal King?
Ans. Akbar

Q8. Munshi Premchand was famous:
Ans. Hindi Writer.

Q9. Elephanta Caves are situated at:
Ans. Maharashtra

Q10. Taj Mahal is made of:
Ans. White Marble

Q11. How many players can play cricket in one team?

Ans. 11

Q12. Yellow and Red makes:
Ans. Orange

Q13. Which Language is known as Universal language?
Ans. English

Q14. "The Last Supper" Painting was made by:
Ans. Leonardo da vinci

Q15. The river which flows adjacent to Red Fort, Delhi is:
Ans. Yamuna

Q16. Name any Movie made by M.F. Husain:
Ans. Gaj Gamini

Q17. The best result for water colour painting is on:
Ans. Paper

Q18. The famous "Madhubani Painting" represents which state of India?
Ans. Bihar

Q19. Which colour is used in the “chakra” of Indian National Flag?
Ans. Blue

Q20. Ajanta Caves are known for:
Ans. Paintings

Q21. Which Indian artist has created the maximum number of images of Indian God?
Ans. Raja Ravi Verma

Q22. Before establishing in Delhi, Jamia Millia Islamia was founded in which city?

Ans. Aligarh

Q23. World famous comedian “Charlie Chaplin” belongs to which country?
Ans. Britain

Q24. India got Independence from British rule in:
Ans. 1947

Q25. The yellow portion of an egg is called:
Ans. Yolk

Q26. "Bani Thani" the famous portrait painting is in which style ?
Ans. Rajasthani style

Q27. "Dancing Girl" the famous sculpture of Mohanjodaro civilization is in which medium?
Ans. Bronze

Q28. Sardar Ballabh Bhai Patel was the leader of which political party in India?
Ans. Indian National Congress Party

Q29. Who headed the making the constitution of India?
Ans. Dr. Bheem Rao Ambedkar

Q30. Amrita Sher-Gill was famous for her:
Ans. Oil colour painting

Q31. Which is the highest peak of Himalaya Mountain?
Ans. Kanchenjunga

Q32. Discovery of India was written by which politician ?
Ans. Pandit Jawaharlal Nehru

Q33. Netaji Subhash Chandra Bose formed an army known as:

Ans. Azad Hind Fauj

Q34. Who was Tyeb Mehta?
Ans. Famous Indian Painter

Q35. To increase hardness, we would select pencils with:
Ans. 2H, 4H, 6H, 7H, 8H Leads

Q36. The classic Ajanta painting belongs to which period?
Ans. Gupta period

Q37. Which artist painted series painting with Madhuri Dixit as the model?
Ans. M.F. Husain

Q38. Which Indian Musician is credited with instrument "Shehnai"?
Ans. Bismillah Khan

Q39. Ajanta caves were discovered in which year?
Ans. 1819

Q40. Who is known for co-founding and chairman of "face book"?
Ans. Mark Zuckerberg

Q41. How many sides does Isosceles triangle have equal?
Ans. 2 equal sides

Q42. Which colour is obtained mixing red and green?
Ans. Brown

Q43. Name any Online Shopping site in India?
Ans. Amazon

Q44. Emerald is a shade of which colour?

Ans. Green

Q45. Neon sign boards is medium of:
Ans. Outdoor advertising

Q46. Pichwai style of folk painting belongs to:
Ans. Rajasthan

Q47. Who Painted "Shakuntala"?
Ans. Raja Ravi Verma

Q48. Straight line that passes through the centre of the circle is called as:
Ans. Diameter

Q49. Name any International Dance form?
Ans. Salsa Dance

Q50. The first Indian awarded the Oscar for lifetime achievements in cinema was:

Ans. Satyajit Ray

Q51. What is “Calligraphy”?
Ans. Art of stylized writing

Q52. Lakshman is famous for:
Ans. His contribution in Cartoon caricature

Q53. Name a pair of complementary colours:
Ans. Blue-Orange

Q54. Sanchi Stupa are situated:
Ans. Near Bhopal

Q55. Horizontal lines suggests:

Ans. Gravity and Stability

Q56. Sculpture "Statue of Liberty" is there in:
Ans. New York City

Q57. "Sonata" car is the model of:
Ans. Hyundai Motors

Q58. "Cinthol" soap is been branded under:
Ans. Godrej

Q59. Rabindranath Tagore have written the National Anthems for:
Ans. India, Bangladesh

Q60. Anish Kapoor is a world famous:
Ans. Sculptor

Q61. The Taj Mahal is on the south bank of which river?
Ans. Yamuna River

Q62. Who is Sankho Chaudhuri?
Ans. Sculptor

Q63. "Gond" painting is popular in which state of India?
Ans. Madhya Pradesh

Q64. Who is the Author of Humayun-Nama?
Ans. Gulbadan Begum

Q65. Tanjore paintings is the native art form of:
Ans. (Thanjavur) Tamil Nadu

Q66. What was the real name of Swami Vivekananda?

Ans. Narendranath Datta

Q68. The folk "Chhau dance" is originated in which part of India?

Ans. West Bengal

Q69. Who composed "Saarey Jahan Sey Acha Hindustaan..."?
Ans. Muhammad Iqbal

Q70. Ikebana is a Japanese art of:
Ans. Flower Arrangements

Q71. The technique of Mural paintings executing freshly laid lime plaster is known as?
Ans. Fresco

Q72. Whose influence was seen in the world of Gandhara School?
Ans. Greek

Q73. Raja Harish Chandra, an early Indian film was produced by?
Ans. Dadasaheb Phalke

Q74. Which colorsare used to show transparency?
Ans. Water Colours

Q75. Which is the softest pencil?
Ans. 10B,12B

Q76. Where is the famous Mona Lisa Painting located?
Ans. The Louvre Museum, Paris

Q77. Which colour is also called earth colour?
Ans. Prussian blue
Q78. Khajuraho Temples are situated at:

Ans. Madhya Pradesh

Q79. The Sistine Chapel is painted by:
Ans. Michelangelo

Q80. Where was India's first civilisation settled?
Ans. Indus Valley

Q81. Chandigarh city design by
Ans. Le- Corbusier

Q82. Name any one Hindi Poet?
Ans. Harivansh Rai Bacchan

Q83. Rabindranath Tagore was born on:
Ans. 7th May 1861

Q84. The distance between two points is called:
Ans. Line

Q.85. The method of Dying clothes by applying wax is known as:

Ans. Batik

Q86. Etching is an intaglio process of:
Ans. Print Making

Q87. Jahangir Art Gallery is situated in:
Ans. Mumbai

Q88. Name any one painting of Van Gogh?
Ans. Sunflower

Q89. Salar Jung Museum is in:

Ans. Telangana

Q90. Wash Paintings belongs to:
Ans. Bengal School

Q91. Pandit Hari Prasad Chorasia was famous for:
Ans. Flute

Q92. Which play is known as the last complete play of Shakespeare?
Ans. The Two Nobel Kinsmen

Q93. Which key is found on the left corner of a standard computer keyboard?
Ans. Escape

Q94. Who won the cricket world cup in the year 2015?
Ans. Australia

Q95. When was M.F Husain born?
Ans. 17th September 1915

Q96. Auguste Robin was a famous:
Ans. Sculptor

Q97. A plane figure with ten side and angles:

Ans. Decagon

Q98. Where was the woodblock printing first started:
Ans. China

Q99. Qawalli music is based on:
Ans. Sufi poetry

Q100. The Desert Festival, on annual event in Rajasthan that displays local folk arts and culture,
aerobatics, camel race, is held at:

Ans. Jaisalmer

Q101. Warli is folk painting of which state?
Ans. Maharashtra

Q102. The Longest River in the world is:
Ans. Nile

Q103. Where is the Statue of Unity situated?
Ans. India, Gujarat

Q104. Line, shape, colour, value, texture, space and form as a group are called the:
Ans. Elements of art

Q105. Louvre Museum is located in:
Ans. Paris

Q106. TAMAS is characterized by which colour?
Ans. Black

Q107. Name the Indian Painter, who was famous for his oil paintings?
Ans. Raja Ravi Verma

Q108. Giant Sculpture of YAKSHA at Reserve Bank of India, New Delhi is the creation of?
Ans. Ram Kinkar Baij

Q109. Who was the best artist of Birds in the court of Jehangir?
Ans. Ustad Mansur

Q110. What is "LOGO"?
Ans. Stylized name of Product Brand

Q111. Who authored "Gitanjali"?

Ans. Rabindranath Tagore

Q112. What is the full form of LED?
Ans. Light Emitting Diode

Q113. Pabuji is related to which state?
Ans. Rajasthan

Q114. What is the tagline of "Jio"?
Ans. Jio Digital Life

Q115. How many lions are there in Ashok Chakra?
Ans. Four lions

Q116. Name the Ex. President of India, who also served as V.C. of Aligarh Muslim University?
Ans. Dr. Zakir Hussain

Q117. Which kind of thing is associated with "Brocade" ?
Ans. Saree (fabric)

Q118. To which country, does the Monalisa, the famous painting belongs?
Ans. France

Q119. The Subject Matter of Ajanta Wall Paintings is:
Ans. Tales of Jatakas (Buddhist)

Q120. Which of the element exist in all Fine-Arts?
Ans. Stylistic Features Ex. (line, space, texture, form, space, colour, and value)

Q121. Who is perceived as the "Father of Modern Art"?
Ans. Paul Cezanne

Q122. Name any Tantric Painter?

Ans. G.R. Santosh

Q123. Poster in comparison to Hoarding is :
Ans. Small

Q124. Stained glass windows, are related to which tradition of painting?
Ans. Gothic Art

Q125. Who painted popular painting "Bharat-Mata"?
Ans. Abanindranath Tagore

Q126. Who wrote Kul-Geet of B.H.U. Varanasi?
Ans. Dr. Shanti Swarup Bhatnagar

Q127. Where was Lord Buddha born?
Ans. Lumbini, Nepal

Q128. Who wrote this patriotic song "Aey Mere Vatan Ke Logo Zara Aankh Mein Bhar
Lo Paani"?

Ans. Pradeep

Q129. Radio Advertisements with rhymes and music are known as:

Ans. Jingles

Q130. Who propounded the theory of Imitation in Art?
Ans. Plato

Q131. In which continent did the "Wood Block Painting" Originate?
Ans. Asia

Q132. What is Graphite?
Ans. Pencil Lead

Q133. Name the popular painting of Kishangarh:
Ans. Bani Thani

Q134. Where is the "Bharat-Bhawan" situated?
Ans. Bhopal

Q135. Who authored "Chitra-Lakshanam"?
Ans. Nagnajit

Q136. Which of the fine arts comes under "3D" Art?
Ans. Sculpture

Q137. In European Painting, name a famous Landscape Painter:
Ans. John Constable

Q138. What's opposite of Relief Painting?
Ans. Intaglio

Q139. Elephanta Caves are famous for:
Ans. Religious Painting

Q140. Name a famous sand sculptor of India:
Ans. Sudarshan Pattnaik

Q141. Which number of Cave of Ajanta has the largest sleeping Buddha Sculptor?
Ans. Cave 26

Q142. A circle has _______ as perimeter:
Ans. Circumference

Q143. "The Hindu" is a:
Ans. Daily Newspaper

Q144. The full form of AMU is:
Ans. Aligarh Muslim University

Q145. Chisel is a tool used for:
Ans. Carving

Q146. Wood Carving is a genre of:
Ans. Sculpture

Q147. Bombay Progressive Artists Group was based in:
Ans. Mumbai

Q148. Taj Mahal is a:
Ans. Mughal Architecture

Q149. The triangle has got:
Ans. Three sides, three angles

Q150. Upanishads is the book on:
Ans. Philosophy

Q151. A cube consists of:
Ans. 6 square

Q152. The "Horizontal" refers to:
Ans. Lines

Q153. Allah Rakha was a notable:
Ans. Classical Musician

Q154. A pipe is a:
Ans. Cylindrical form

Q155. Rectangle has got:
Ans. 4 sides

Q156. Bhimbetka is famous for:
Ans. Rock Art

Q157. "Sun Temple" of konark is situated in:
Ans. Odisha

Q158. Octagon has got:
Ans. 8 sides

Q159. Who is Faiz Ahmad Faiz?
Ans. Poet

Q160. Ustad Amjad Ali Khan is a notable:
Ans. Musician

Q161. "Quick Heal" is a name of:
Ans. Antivirus software for computer

Q.161 Ellora caves are located in:
Ans. Maharashtra

Q.162 Taj Mahal was constructed by:
Ans. Shahajahan

Q.163 Advertising design is known as:
Ans. Applied Art

Q164. He is a world famous artist:
Ans. Picasso

Q.165 Creation of cup and saucer is a job of:
Ans. Ceramics

Q.166 "Shiva Maheshmurti" also known as "Trimurti" is situated in:
Ans. Elephanta

Q.167 He is famous painter of India:
Ans. Raja Ravi Verma

Q.168 Creation of Adam is painted by:
Ans. Michelangelo

Q.169 Monalisa is famous for:
Ans. Her smile

Q.170 Photoshop is a term connected to:
Ans. Computer operation

Q.171 Ajanta Caves depict stories of:
Ans. Buddhish religion

Q.172 Buland Darwaja is at:
Ans. Agra

Q.173 Gateway of India is at:
Ans. Mumbai

Q.174 Padmapani Bodhiattva is a:
Ans. Painting

Q.175 Temple Kailash is situated at:
Ans. Ellora

Q.176 Poster colours are:
Ans. Water based

Q.177 The sculpture of Natraj depicts God:
Ans. Shiva

Q.178 Cool Colours are:
Ans. Blue, Violet, Green

Q.179 The figure guarding the temple door are called:
Ans. Dwarapala

Q.180 Top portion of temple is called:
Ans. Shikhara

Q.181 Cyberspace is known as:
Ans. Computer Centre

Q.182 Leonardo da vinci has painted:
Ans. The Last Supper

Q.183 Monitor is related with:
Ans. Computer

Q.184 Bahubali is at:
Ans. Shravanabelagola

Q.185 Kalidasa is a:
Ans. Poet

Q.186 Gopuram is connected with:
Ans. Temple

Q.187 Warli painting is a tribal art of:
Ans. India

Q.188 Miniature paintings are:
Ans. Small Paintings

Q.189 The photographs in the book are called:
Ans. Pictures

Q.190 This animal is transformed in a famous cartoon character:
Ans. Mouse, bear, cat

Q.191 Quickly done drawing is called:
Ans. Sketch

Q.192 Shape is _________ dimensional.
Ans. Two dimensional

Q.193 Coloured glass painting is called:
Ans. Stain glass painting

Q.194 A method to show distance in painting is called:
Ans. Perspective

Q.195 When one light ray is passed through prism we see:
Ans. Seven Colours

Q.196 A technique in which coloured stones are used to create a picture on the wall:
Ans. Stone work (Pietra Dura)

Q.197 Egyptians have created__________ to keep the dead bodies of kings and queens.
Ans. Pyramids

Q.198 Which animal is associated with Lord Shiva?
Ans. Bull

Q.199 In Jain religion, spiritual teachers are called:
Ans. Tirthankara

Q.200 Black Colour + White colour give us:
Ans. Grey

Q.201 Red, Yellow and Blue on colour wheel are:
Ans. Primary colours

Q.202 First person to discover the existence of colours in light itself is:
Ans. Sir Isaac Newton

Q.203 Colour which indicates "GO" in Traffic Signal is:
Ans. Green

Q.204 We can see any object with the help of:
Ans. Light and vision

Q.205 One Centimetre is equal to:
Ans. 10 mm

Q.206 One foot is equal to:
Ans. 12 inches

Q.207 The art of beautiful handwriting is called:
Ans. Calligraphy

Q.208 Following is a output device of computer:
Ans. Printer

Q.209 When someone watches something carefully is called:
Ans. Observation

Q.210 A painting of Padmapani Buddha is painted in:
Ans. Ajanta Caves

Q.211 Sir J.J School of Art is situated in:
Ans. Mumbai

Q.212 Dr. Jayant Narlikar is a:
Ans. Astrophysicist

Q.213 M.F Hussain is a famous:
Ans. Painter

Q.214 India gate is situate in:
Ans. New Delhi

Q.215 A first Scientist who became president of India:
Ans. Dr. A.P.J Abdul Kalam

Q.216 B.F.A Degree of University of Mumbai is given by:
Ans. Mumbai University

Q.217 A Picture produced with camera is called:
Ans. Photograph

Q.218 A tool that you use to paint is a:
Ans. Brush

Q.219 Medium of Poster colour is:
Ans. Water

Q.220 The measurement or distance of something from one to the other is called:
Ans. Length

Q.221 A curved piece of glass in camera is:
Ans. Lens

Q.222 The skill of designing building is:
Ans. Architecture

Q.223 The study of beauty especially in art is called:
Ans. Aesthetics

Q.224 It's flying:

Ans. Right to Left

Q.225 A and B are:

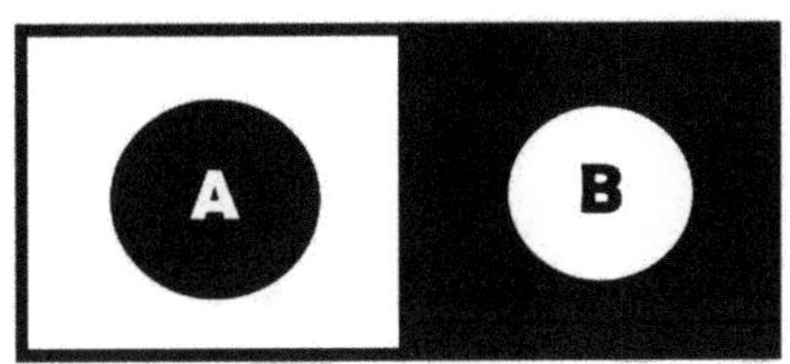

Ans. ‘A’ and ‘B’ are equal

Q.226 This is a:

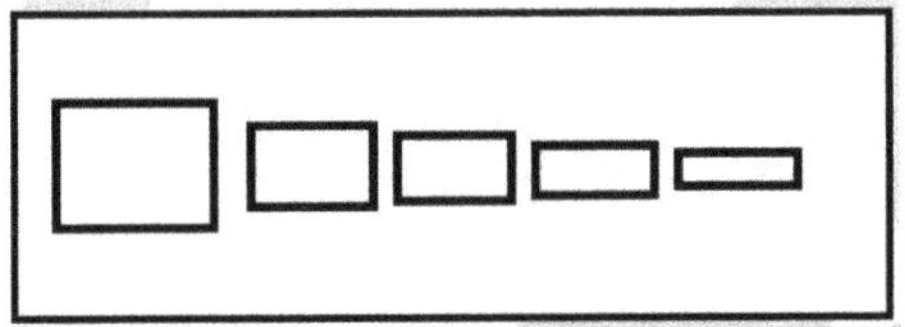

Ans. Gradation

Q.227 This is a:

Ans. Replica

Q.228 This is a graphic presentation of:

Enter Caption

Ans. Eye

Q.229 This is a :

Ans. Repetition

Q.230 This is:

Enter Caption

Ans. Symmetrical Balance

Q.231 This is:

Enter Caption

Ans. Raining

Q.232 This is Symbolic Presentation of:

Ans. Handicape

Q.233 His is a Symbolic Presentation of:

Enter Caption

Ans. Peace

Q.234 You can get colour green by mixing _________
Ans. Yellow and Blue

Q.235 Colour Red suggests _________
Ans. Danger

Q.236 Which one of the following is not a primary colour?
Ans. Black

Q.237 _________ Joins two points by shortest distance.
Ans. A straight line

Q.238 A serif is part of_________

Ans. Letterform

Q.239 Interior designer designs _________
Ans. Homes

Q.240 The hard pencils are of _________
Ans. H grades

Q.241 Lata Mangeshkar is a well-known:
Ans. Singer

Q.242 Elephanta Caves are situated near:
Ans. Mumbai

Q.243 Ajanta caves are situated near:
Ans. Aurangabad (Maharashtra)

Q.244 'Warli' painting is a:
Ans. Tribal Art of Maharashtra

Q.245 The Degree B.F.A stands for:
Ans. Bachelor of Fine Art

Q.246 Calligraphy is an art of
Ans. Beautiful Handwriting

Q.247 Which Software is used for generating images?
Ans. Corel Draw

Q.248 Restaurant is suggested by which symbol?
Ans.

Enter Caption

Q.249 The three primary colours on the colour wheel are red, blue and _________
Ans. Yellow

Q.250 Where did water colour painting started in 18th century?
Ans. England

Q.251 The main festival of Maharashtra is:
Ans. Ganesh Chaturthi

Q.252 Olympics 2008 were held in:
Ans. Beijing

Q.253 Konark is well known for its:
Ans. Sun Temple

Q.254 What is the folk dance of Gujarat?
Ans. Garba

Q.255 The city discovered in the Indus Civilization is:

Ans. Mohen-jo-daro

Q.256 The colour of the chakra (wheel) of the Indian National Flag is:
Ans. Navy Blue

Q.257 The highest civilian honour of the country is:
Ans. Bharat Ratna

Q.258 Sania Mirza is associated with which sport?
Ans. Tennis

Q.259 Kathakali is the dance form of:
Ans. Kerala

Q.260 He was a well-known Marathi author:

Ans. Puroshottam Laxman Deshpande

Q.261 Padmapani Bodhisatva is a famous painting at:
Ans. Ajanta Caves

Q.262 Mahavira is associated with which religion?
Ans. Jainism

Q.263 The following is the input device of a computer:
Ans. Mouse

Q.264 One inch is equal to:
Ans. 2.54 cm

Q.265 The music director who won the Oscar for Slumdog Millionaire is:
Ans. A.R. Rahman

Q.266 This is the hardest pencil:

Ans. 10 H

Q.267 Satyajit Ray is a famous:
Ans. Film maker

Q.268 The Gol Gumbaz is situated in:
Ans. Bijapur

Q.269 Salar Jung museum is situated in:
Ans. Hyderabad

Q.270 The standard unit of measuring distance is:
Ans. Kilometer

Q.271 Famous cartoon Characters of Walt Disney is:
Ans. Mickey Mouse

Q.272 Satish Gujral is a famous:
Ans. Artist

Q.273 He was the first President of India:
Ans. Dr. Rajendra Prasad

Q.274 This is a symbol of:

Enter Caption

Ans. State Bank of India

Q.275 This character was created by:

Ans. R.K Laxman

Q.276 How many triangles are there in all?

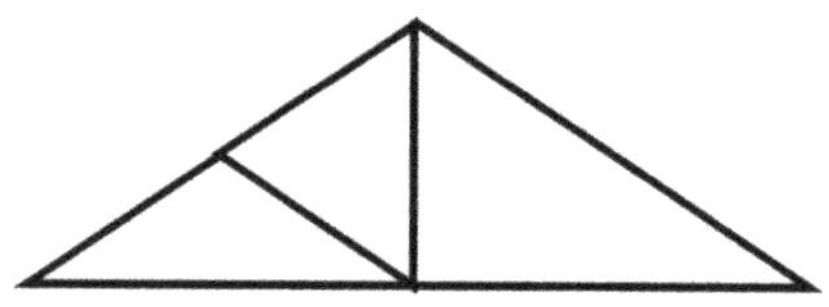

Ans. Five

Q.277 This is called:

Ans. Repetition

Q.278 This is the part situated in CPU:
Ans. Mother board

Q.279 Power supply in computer is regulated by:
Ans. SMPS

Q.280 R.K Laxman is a:
Ans. Cartoonist Artist

Q.281 Navratan Himani Hair Oil is endorsed by:
Ans. Amitabh Bachhan

Q.282 'Jahangir Art gallery is located at:

Ans. Mumbai

Q.283 M.F. Hussain has been offered the citizenship of:
Ans. Qatar

Q.284 Bharat Natyam is a dance form of:
Ans. Tamil Nadu

Q. 285 Secondary colours are formed with the combination of:
Ans. Primary

Q.286 The Primary colours are:
Ans. Red, Blue, Yellow

Q.287 The warm colours are:
Ans. Red, yellow, orange and Saffron

Q.288 Colours are perceived by:
Ans. Light, eye and mind

Q.289 India Gate is located at:
Ans. Delhi

Q.290 Ajmal kasab is convicted for:
Ans. 9/11 attacks

Q.291 In Pakistan POK is known as:
Ans. Pak Occupied Kashmir

Q.292 Hema Malini is a _________ dancer.
Ans. Bharat Natayam

Q.293 Who is involved with the logo of RK films:

Ans. Raj Kapoor

Q.294 I-pod is used for:
Ans. Music

Q.295 SMS stands for:

Ans. Short message service

Q.296 In1955 which painting of Hussain was awarded the Lalit Kala Academy national award?
Ans. Zameen

Q.297 Mumbai's International Airport is named after:
Ans. Chhatrapati Shivaji

Q.298 During the reign of Akbar, Dhrupad Singers included:
Ans. Tansen

Q.299 Udaipur is known as:
Ans. Sun City

Q.300 IPL"s sacked commissioner was

Ans. Lalit Kr. Modi

Q.301 Where did Fresco technique mainly used between 14th to 16th century?
Ans. Italy

Q.302 Nagpur is known as:
Ans. Orange

Q.303 Vijay Mallya was the owner of IPL team of:
Ans. Royal Challengers

Q.304 The point where the lines come together on the horizon is:

Ans. Vanishing point

Q.305 The specific qualities of being a poet, author, and an artist belongs to which person?
Ans. Rabindranath Tagore

Q.306 The Logo of the company „Apple" was designed by:
Ans. Rob Janoff

Q.307 Where did water colour painting started in 18th century?
Ans. England

Q.308 Where did Fresco technique mainly used between 14th to 16th century?
Ans. Italy

Q.309 Which material is not used in oil Painting?
Ans. Water

Q.310 The point where the lines come together on the horizon is:
Ans. Vanishing point

Q.311 What is Monochrome?
Ans. Tones of one colour

Q.312 Who is the Dierctor of Kiran Nadar Museum of Art?
Ans. Roobina Karode

Q.313 The specific qualities of being a poet, author, and an artist belongs to which person?
Ans. Rabindranath Tagore

Q.314 During the reign of Akbar , Dhrupad Singers included:
Ans. Tansen

Q.315 Gutam Bhuddha gave his first sermon at-

Ans. Sarnath

Q.316 Vansthali Vidyapeeth is mainly known as successful experiment in the field of –
Ans. Women Education

Q.317 Teleconferencing is best suited in-
Ans. Face to face teaching

Q.318 Dilwara Temple is situated in
Ans. Mount Abu

Q.319 „Wings of life" is a famous Autobiography of
Ans. A.P.J Abdul kalam

Q.320 Anupam sood is a famous
Ans. Print maker

Q.321 Sanchi Stupa was built in
Ans. Mauryan Period

Q.322 Which city is called "the city of lakes"
Ans. Udaipur

Q.323 This is a

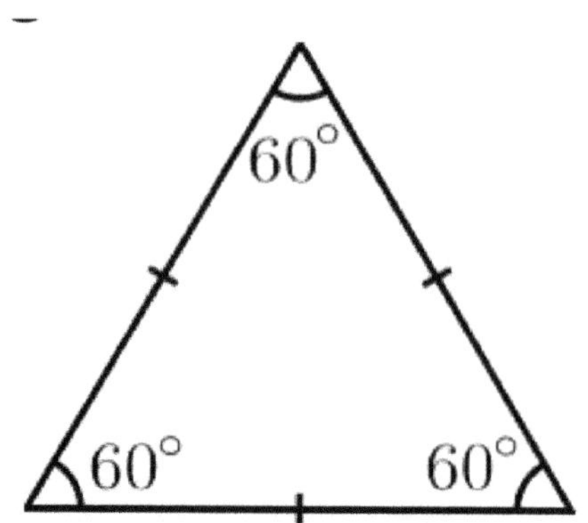

Ans. Equilateral Triangle

Q.324 National School of drama is situated in which city
Ans. New Delhi

Q.325 "The School of Athens" is famous painting made by
Ans. Raphael

Q.326 „President of India
Ans. Sh. Draupadi Murmu ji

Q.327 British Prince Williams was recently married to

Ans. Catherine Middleton

Q.328 The capital of Ladakh is
Ans. Leh

Q.329 Golden Temple in Amritsar Punjab is surrounded by
Ans. Water

Q.330 Speaker of LokSabha is
Ans. Meira Kumar

Q.331 Vivekananda Rock is in the
Ans. South of India

Q.332 The ruling party in Gujarat state is
Ans. BJP

Q.333 „Sericulture" is a study of
Ans. Silkworms

Q.334 The name of the State Emporium of Handicrafts and Handlooms of Andhra
Pradesh is

Ans. Lepakshi

Q.335 The most famous food item during Ramzan month in Hyderabad is
Ans. Haleem

Q.336 Rabindranath Tagore won the Nobel Prize for his collection of poems called
Ans. Gitanjali

Q.337 The New Chief Minister of Tamil Nadu is
Ans. Edappadi K. Palaniswami

Q.338 Which Renaissance artist painted one of the world"s most famous painting,
Monalisa?
Ans. Leonardo da Vinci

Q.339 Pyramids were constructed by Egyptian Kings for the purpose of
Ans. Burying the dead royal family members

Q.340 „Cave Paintings" were done during
Ans. Pre Historic Times

Q.341 „Hampi Vijaynagar" is famous for
Ans. Sculptures and Monuments

Q.342 „Posters" are used for
Ans. Publicity Purpose/Information to all in General

Q.343 „Raja Ravi Varma" was a well known
Ans. Painter

Q.345 The colours (dyes) used in Kalamkari paintings and block prints are made from
Ans. Vegetable & minerals

Q.346 Kondapalli toys Handicrafts industry is located in
Ans. Krishna district

Q.347 Taj Mahal was built in the memory of
Ans. Mumtaz

Q.348 Thousand Pillar Temple is situated in
Ans. Warangal

Q.349 „Borra caves" are located near

Ans. Vishakhapatnam

Q.350 Calligraphy means
Ans. Beautiful handwriting

Q.351 Sistine Chapel ceiling paintings were painted by
Ans. Michelangelo

Q.352 Folk Arts are the art forms of
Ans. Tribals

Q.353 „Art" is a form of
Ans. Self-Expression

Q.354 .... will captain the college team?
Ans. Who

Q.355 Political leaders should think of the people .... They are accountable.
Ans. To whom

Q.356 Gandhiji used .... major part of his time for spinning
Ans. a

Q.357 He is .... Right man for the job.
Ans. the

Q.358 Fragile means ....
Ans. Delicate

Q.359 The antonym of timid is
Ans. Adventurous

Q.360 The antonym of diligent is

Ans. Idle

Q.361 Abortive is the synonym of..........
Ans. Futile

Q.362 Fratricide means the murder of one"s ....
Ans. Brother

Q.363 The first person who .... the question will be awarded a prize.
Ans. Answers

Q.364 I hope you succeed ....your effort.
Ans. In

Q.365 Always be ....
Ans. Honest

Q.366 Tom has .... English lessons on Thursdays
Ans. His

Q.367 This film is .... than his last one
Ans. Better

Q.368 I am fair .... my sister is dark
Ans. But

Q.369 Which is a Hotcolour?
Ans. Red

Q.370 Taking impression from stone the process is called?
Ans. Planography printing

Q.371 First book printed form wood block in?

Ans. China

Q.372 What is multimedia?
Ans. Computer

Q.373 The national emblem of india is based on?
Ans. The Ashokan lion capital at Sarnath

Q.374 Central Lalit Kala Academy has established zonal centre is one of these cities?
Ans. Delhi

Q.375 Elephanta is famous for?
Ans. Trimurt

Q.376 Bengal school paintings are known for their one of these qualities?
Ans. Wash technique

Q.377 NIFT is an educational centre devoted to?
Ans. Fashion technology

Q.378 Maximum size of the Hoarding is?
Ans. 20`x 60'

Q.379 Poster is comparison to Hoarding?
Ans. Smalle

Q.380 Size of press ad indicated by?
Ans. Column

Q.381 First Poster designer was?
Ans. Henri de Toulouse-Lautrec

Q.382 One inch has -----------?

Ans. 72 points

Q.383 The cloth used in silk screen making?
Ans. Bolting Cloth

Q.384 Letter press printing come under process?
Ans. Relief Printing

Q.385 Where did kabirdas attain "NIRVANA"?
Ans. Maghar

Q.386 Where the colour T.V. was introduced in India?
Ans. 1982

Q.387 How many colours are in a "Rainbow"
Ans. Seven

Q.388 The Madhubani Paintings belong to one of these state?
Ans. Bihar

Q.389 Ashokan Pillar was made of?
Ans. Red sand stone

Q.390 What are the jataka tales?
Ans. Previous birth stories of Buddha

Q.391 The most important factor for painting is?
Ans. Good paper

Q.392 The Ajanta paintings belong to the?
Ans. Gupta period

Q.393 Pongal is popular festival of which state?

Ans. Tamilnadu

Q.394 Who wrote "Vande Matram"?
Ans. Bankim Chandr

Q.395 Moveable types were invented by?
Ans. Bi Sheng

Q.396 In computer terminology a "floppy disk" is a?
Ans. Device for data

Q.397 Which of the galleries has the largest collection of the Raja Ravi Verma"s
Paintings?
Ans. Chitra Art Gallery Trivendram

Q.398 Basic color is?
Ans. Blue

Q.399 Painting made of paper cuttings is known as?
Ans. Collage picture

Q.400 "Osama Bin Laden" was shot dead in
Ans. Pakistan

Q.401 Faculty of Fine Arts, JMI has
Ans. Six Department

Q.402 Who wrote "Godaan" novel?
Ans. Munshi Prem Chand

Q.403 Which of the following light source is most efficient
Ans. LED

Q.404 Data going in computer is called
Ans. Input

Q.405 RAM stands for
Ans. Random Access memory

Q.406 The Space Agency NASA belongs to
Ans. U.S

Q.407 Which among the following is a source of non-conventional source of energy?
Ans. Solar Power

Q.408 The largest continent in term of Area is:
Ans. Asia

Q.409 A document layout where the width is greater than the height
Ans. Landscape

Q.410 The Election Commission of India is situated in?
Ans. New Delhi

Q.411 In Field Hockey, each team has.....players on the field at any one time.

Ans. 11

Q.412 Where is the Statue of Liberty located?
Ans. New York, U.S

Q.413 Where is the famous Mona Lisa painting located today
Ans. Musee De Lourve, Paris

Q.414 Paper making originated in
Ans. China

Q.415 The National bird of India is;
Ans. Peacock

Q.416 Which country"s national game is Hockey?
Ans. India

Q.417 Which bird is the symbol of Peace
Ans. Dove

Q.418 The Biggest Book Store is:
Ans. Oxford

Q.419 Jai Gangajal film is directed by
Ans. Prakash Jha

Q.420 Who made "Kalighat Paintings"
Ans. Jamini Roy

Q.421 Which famous explorer visited India in the late 13th century?
Ans. Marco Polo

Q.422 Who was honoured by the prestigious Dada SahebPhalke award in 2015
Ans. Shashi Kapoor

Q.423 6B Pencils are
Ans. Very Soft

Q.424 „Lavani" is the famous Dance of
Ans. Maharashtra

Q.425 "Connecting India" tag line belongs to
Ans. BSNL

Q.426 What does LPG stand for?
Ans. Gas

Q.427 Lucknow embroidery is known as
Ans. Chikankari Embroidery

Q.428 Which is most famous Painting of Picasso
Ans. Guernica

Q.429 Which company''s name is based on river''s name?
Ans. Nokia

Q.430 The term "PC" stands for,
Ans. Personal Computer

Q.431 Painter KG Subramanian is from which state
Ans. Kerala

Q.432 Pulak Biswas belongs to
Ans. Book Illustration

Q.433 Which medium takes the most time to dry?
Ans. Oil

Q.434 Indian cosmetics products are from?
Ans. Hindustan Liver

Q.435 What is the average font size used in a book?
Ans. 12 pts

Q.436 Where is the Victoria Memorial Hall located?
Ans. Kolkata

Q.437 Which word belongs to Tracking and Kerning?
Ans. Typography

Q.438 Which film wins 89th Academy Awards for best picture?
Ans. Moonlight

Q.439 Who was known a greatest Indian filmmakers of the 20th century?
Ans. Satyajit Ray

Q.440 Violet is made by the mixing of....
Ans. Blue + Red

Q.441 Who was the superstar of the Pop Art movement?
Ans. Andy Warhol

Q.442 JWT is name of the....
Ans. Advertising agency

Q.443 Which monument is not UNESCO World Heritage Site?
Ans. Tughlaqabad Fort

Q.444 Who is the winner of 64th National Film Awards for best actor in 2017?
Ans. Akshay Kumar

Q.445 Which software doesn"t belong to Adobe Creative Suit?
Ans. Corel Draw

Q.446 Tagline "The taste of India is related with....
Ans. Amul

Q.447 Ctrl + A command stands for
Ans. Select all

Q.448 "Taste Bhi, Health Bhi" is associated with.....
Ans. Maggi

Q.449 Poster colour is............ Medium
Ans. Opaque

Q.450 A pencil marked "HH" is........
Ans. Very hard

Q.451 Notre Dame Cathedral is known for its.....
Ans. French Gothic architecture

Q.452 Who made the famous Scuplture "Snthal Family"?
Ans. Ramkinkar Baij

Q.453 Which is the highest civilian award of the Republic of India?
Ans. Bharat Ratna award

Q.454 Who was the architect of India Gate?
Ans. Edwin Lutyens

Q.455 Who is the New Global Brand Ambassador of L"Oreal Paris?
Ans. Deepika Padukone

Q.456 Morarto is.........

Ans. Online Shoping Browser

Q.457 What is the full form of ATM?

Ans. Automated Teller Machine

Q.458 The meaning of Bauhaus is.........
Ans. School of Building

Q.459 PusarlaVentaka Sindhu is..........
Ans. Badminton player

Q.460 Kruti Dev is name of the..........
Ans. Hindi font

Q.461 Centre Pompidou is situated in.........
Ans. France

Q.462 Processor of computer generates
Ans. Heat

Q.463 Hindustan Uniliver is known as a
Ans. FMCG

Q.464 Carbon used ribbon is essential part of
Ans. Dot Matrix printer

Q.465 A collection of historical documents that provide information about the past is
Ans. Archive

Q.466 A period of time when teacher teaches people is

Ans. Lesson

Q.467 The twin cities of Hyderabad and Secunderabad are connected by
Ans. Hussainsagar lake

Q.468 Original name of Poster?
Ans. Bill board

Q.469 This animal is NOT associated with ten incarnations of Vishnu
Ans. Godzilla

Q.470 When was the Ministry of Environmental, forest and climate change formed?
Ans. 1985

THANK YOU

BEST WISHES FOR YOU

www.ingramcontent.com/pod-product-compliance
Lightning Source LLC
LaVergne TN
LVHW070843160826
845684LV00008B/60

* 9 7 9 8 8 9 4 7 5 5 7 3 1 *